The Felt Formula

Felting is not a precise science. Wool felts when exposed to water, heat and agitation, but each element is hard to control precisely. As a result, each individual garment may vary in the way it felts.

Felting can be done in the sink, but washing machines get the job done more quickly. Each washing machine is different, and the amount your machine felts a piece after one cycle may vary from your neighbors', so be sure to follow the specific felting instructions of the piece you are making. Check your piece a few times during your felting process to make sure you are getting the desired results.

The felting process releases fibers which can clog your washing machine. Therefore, you may want to place items to be felted in a roomy mesh bag before putting them in the washing machine. Also, adding other laundry when felting will increase the amount of agitation and speed up the process. Be careful, though, to use items that won't shed fibers of their own (such as jeans).

Felting Facts

Felting a knit or crochet piece makes it shrink. Therefore, the piece you knit or crochet must start out much bigger than the finished felted size will be. How much will it shrink? Good question. Shrinkage varies since there are so many factors that affect it. These variables include water temperature, th (and how long) the pi type of soap used, yarn brand and color.

You can control how much your piece felts by watching it closely. Check your piece after about ten minutes to see how quickly it is felting. Look at the stitch definition and size to determine if the piece has been felted enough.

How to Felt

Place items to be felted in the washing machine along with one tablespoon of detergent and a pair of jeans or other laundry. (Remember, do not wash felting with other clothing that releases its own fibers.) Set washing machine on smallest load using hot water. Start machine and check progress after ten minutes. Check progress more frequently after piece starts to felt. Reset the machine if needed to continue the agitation cycle. As the piece becomes more felted, you may need to pull it into shape. When the piece has felted to the desired size, rinse it by hand in warm water. Remove the excess water either by rolling in a towel and squeezing, or in the spin cycle of your washing machine. Block the piece into shape, and let air dry. For pieces that need to conform to a particular shape (such as a hat or purse), it may be helpful to stuff the piece with a towel to help it hold its shape while drying.

For more information on felting with the yarns used in this book, visit www.lionbrand.com.

Before

After

Keep-Warm Slippers

EASY

Finished Sizes

Instructions given fit woman's shoe size 6-7 *(small)* after felting; changes for shoe sizes 8-9 *(medium)* and 10-11 *(large)* after felting are in [ ].

Materials

- Lion Brand Landscapes super bulky (super chunky) weight yarn (1¾ oz/55 yds/50g per ball):
  3 [4, 5] balls #271 rose garden
- Size H/8/5mm crochet hook or size needed to obtain gauge
- Tapestry needle
- 2 yds ⅝-inch-wide dusty rose grosgrain ribbon
- Cardboard

Gauge

With 1 strand of yarn: 12 sc = 4 inches

Instructions

Slipper

Make 2.

Sole

Rnd 1: With 2 strands held tog, ch 17 [21, 27]; 3 sc in 2nd ch from hook; sc in next 14 [18, 24] chs, 3 sc in last ch; working in unused lps on opposite side of beg ch, sc in next 14 [18, 24] lps; join in first sc. *(34 [42, 54] sc)*

Rnd 2: Ch 1, 2 sc in each of first 3 sc; sc in next 14 [18, 24] sc, 2 sc in each of next 3 sc; sc in last 14 [18, 24] sc; join in first sc. *(40 [48, 60] sc)*

Rnd 3: Ch 1, 2 sc in each of first 7 sc; sc in next 4 [6, 8] sc, hdc in next 4 [6, 8] sc, dc in next 4 [4, 6] sc, 2 dc in each of next 8 sc; dc in next 4 [4, 6] sc, hdc in next 4 [6,8] sc, sc in next 4 [6, 8] sc, 2 sc in last sc; join in first sc. *(56 [64, 76] sts)*

Fasten off.

Upper Section

Note: *Upper Section is worked with 1 strand only.*

Rnd 1: Join in 7th st of rnd 3; ch 1, sc in same st and in next 15 [19, 25] sts, hdc in next 6 sts, dc in next 12 sts, hdc in next 6 sts, sc in next 16 [20, 26] sts; join in first sc. *(56 [64, 76] sts)*

Rnd 2: Ch 1, sc in same sc and in next 15 [19, 25] sc, hdc in next 6 hdc, dc in next 12 dc, hdc in next 6 hdc, sc in next 16 [20, 26] sc; join in first sc.

Rnd 3: Rep rnd 2.

Note: *For sc dec, draw up lp in 2 sts indicated, yo and draw through all 3 lps on hook.*

Rnd 4: Ch 1, sc in same sc and in next 21 [25, 31] sts, [sc dec *(see Note)* in next 2 sts] 6 times; sc in last 22 [26, 32] sts; join in first sc. *(50 [58, 70] sc)*

Rnd 5: Ch 1, sc in each sc; join in first sc.

Rnd 6: Ch 4 *(counts as a dc and a ch-1 sp)*, sk next sc, dc in next sc; *ch 1, sk next sc, dc in next sc; rep from * to last sc; ch 1, sk last sc; join in 3rd ch of beg ch-4.

Fasten off and weave in ends.

Felting

Note: *Refer to How to Felt on page 1 for additional information.*

Wash by machine on a hot wash/cold rinse cycle with detergent and several pieces of clothing to agitate. To felt additionally, dry by machine on a regular setting until almost dry. Remove from dryer and pull into shape.

Finishing

Ribbon-Trimmed Slippers

Cut ribbon in half. Beg at center front, weave 1 length through ch-1 sps on rnd 6. Pull to tighten and tie in a bow. Rep on other Slipper. Trim ends at an angle.

Pompom-Trimmed Slippers

Tie
Make 2.

Leaving 4-inch end, ch 100; fasten off, leaving 4-inch end. Weave in other end.

Beg at center front, weave 1 Tie through ch-1 sps on rnd 6. Pull to tighten and tie in a bow. Rep on other Slipper.

Pompom
Make 2.

Cut piece of cardboard 3 inches wide. Wrap yarn around cardboard (the more wraps, the fuller the Pompom will be). Cut yarn and carefully slide yarn off cardboard. Cut 18-inch piece of yarn and double it; carefully slide it under center of yarn and tie tightly with double knot. Clip lps, fluff out Pompom, and trim. Attach Pompom to center front of each Slipper.

Ragg Bag

EASY

Finished Size
Approximately 11 inches at bottom, 8 inches at top, 9 inches tall after felting; size will vary depending on amount of felting

Materials
- Lion Brand Lion Wool medium (worsted) weight yarn (3 oz/158 yds/85g per ball): 5 balls #099 winter white *(A)* 4 balls #153 ebony *(B)*
- Size N/13/9mm crochet hook or size needed to obtain gauge
- Tapestry needle
- Sewing needle and matching thread
- Snap closure

Gauge
With 1 strand of A and B held tog: 8 sc = 4 inches

Instructions
Bottom
Row 1: With 1 strand of A and B held tog, ch 28; sc in 2nd ch from hook and in each rem ch, turn. *(27 sc)*

Row 2: Ch 1, sc in each sc, turn.

Rows 3–6: Rep row 2. Fasten off.

Sides
First Side
Row 1: Hold Bottom with 1 short end at top and beg ch to right; with 1 strand of A and B held tog, join in end of row 4; ch 1, working in ends of row, sc in same row and in next 2 rows; working across row 6, sc in each sc; working across next side in ends of rows, sc in row 6 and in next 2 rows, turn. *(33 sc)*

Row 2: Ch 1, sc in each sc, turn.

Rows 3 & 4: Rep row 2.

Note: For **sc dec**, draw up lp in 2 sts indicated, yo and draw through all 3 lps on hook.

Row 5: Ch 1, **sc dec** *(see Note)* in first 2 sc; sc in each sc to last 2 sc; sc dec in last 2 sc, turn. *(31 sc)*

Rows 6–8: Rep row 2.

Row 9: Rep row 5. *(29 sc)*

Rows 10–25: [Work rows 6–9] 4 times. *(21 sc at end of row 25)*

Rows 26–28: Rep row 2.

Fasten off.

2nd Side
Row 1: Hold Bottom with beg ch to left; with 1 strand of A and B held tog, join in end of row 3; ch 1, working in ends of row, sc in same row and in next 2 rows; working in across next side in unused lps of beg ch, sc in each lp; working across next side in ends of rows, sc in row 1 and in next 2 rows, turn. *(33 sc)*

Rows 2–28: Rep rows 2–28 of First Side.

Weave in all ends.

Assembly
With RS facing you and with 1 strand of A and B held tog, sl st ends of Sides tog.

Tab
Row 1: With 1 strand of A and B held tog, ch 4; sc in 2nd ch from hook and in each rem ch, turn. *(3 sc)*

Row 2: Ch 1, sc in each sc, turn.

Rows 3–11: Rep row 2.

Edging
Ch 1, 3 sc in first sc; sc in next sc, 3 sc in next sc, turn Tab to work along long side edge; sc evenly along long edge; 3 sc in next corner; sc in center ch, 3 sc in next corner; sc evenly along rem long edge; join in first sc. Fasten off.

Strap
Row 1: With 1 strand of A and B held tog, ch 2; sc in 2nd ch from hook, turn.

Row 2: Ch 1, sc in sc, turn.

Rep row 2 until piece measures 25 inches.

Fasten off and weave in ends.

Felting
Note: *Refer to How to Felt on page 1 for additional information.*

Turn Bag inside out. Place Bag, Strap and Tab in washer. Wash in hot water wash/cold water rinse/heavy cycle for about 24 minutes wash cycle.

Turn RS out. Lay Strap and Tab flat to dry. Stuff Bag with plastic so bottom edge is flat with sides rising from bottom. Let dry completely.

Finishing
With sewing needle and matching thread, sew Tab on center front of 1 side of Bag. Sew snap closure on other side of Tab and top center of Bag. Sew ends of Strap to inside Bag at each side edge.

Tricolor Tote

EASY

Finished Size

Approximately 10¾ x 12¾ inches after felting

Materials

- Lion Brand Landscapes super bulky (super chunky) weight yarn (1¾ oz/55 yds/50g per ball):
  2 balls each #282 river crossing *(A)*, #275 autumn trails *(B)*, #273 spring desert *(C)*
- Size N/13/9mm crochet hook or size needed to obtain gauge
- Tapestry needle
- Sewing needle and matching thread

SUPER BULKY

Gauge

8 sc = 4 inches before felting

Instructions

Side

Make 2.

Row 1: With A, ch 28; sc in 2nd ch from hook and in each rem ch, turn. *(27 sc)*

Row 2: Ch 1, sc in each sc, turn.

Rows 3–12: Rep row 2. At end of row 12, change to B by drawing lp through; cut A.

Rows 13–24: Rep row 2. At end of row 24, change to C by drawing lp through; cut B.

Rows 25–36: Rep row 2.

Fasten off and weave in all ends.

Strap

With 1 strand of A, B and C held tog, ch 100.

Fasten off and weave in ends.

Assembly

With WS facing you, sl st Sides tog along long sides and 1 short end. With sewing needle and matching thread, sew 1 end of Strap to inside of either side of bag, along side seam. Sew rem end to opposite side along opposite seam.

Felting

Note: *Refer to How to Felt on page 1 for additional information.*

Turn RS out. Wash by machine on a hot wash/cold rinse cycle with detergent and several pieces of clothing to agitate. To felt additionally, dry by machine on a regular setting until almost dry. Remove from dryer and pull into shape.

Furry Floor Rug

EASY

Finished Size

Approximately 33 inches in diameter after felting; size will vary depending on amount of felting

Materials

- Lion Brand Fishermen's Wool medium (worsted) weight yarn (8 oz/465 yds/117 g per skein):
  2 skeins #098 natural *(A)*

4 MEDIUM

- Lion Brand Fun Fur bulky (chunky) weight yarn (1¾ oz/60 yds/50g per ball):
  6 balls #098 ivory *(B)*
  3 balls each #133 tangerine *(C)* and #132 olive green *(D)*

5 BULKY

- Size N/13/9mm crochet hook or size needed to obtain gauge
- Tapestry needle

Gauge

With 1 strand of A and B held tog: 8 dc = 4 inches

Instructions

Rnd 1: With 1 strand of A and B held tog, ch 4; 10 dc in 4th ch from hook *(beg 3 sk chs count as a dc)*; join in 3rd ch of beg ch. *(11 dc)*

Rnd 2: Ch 3 *(counts as a dc on this and following rnds)*, dc in same ch; 2 dc in each rem dc; join in 3rd ch of beg ch-3. *(22 dc)*

Rnd 3: Ch 3, 2 dc in next dc; *dc in next dc, 2 dc in next dc; rep from * around; join in 3rd ch of beg ch-3. *(33 dc)*

Rnd 4: Ch 3, dc in next dc, 2 dc in next dc; *dc in next 2 dc, 2 dc in next dc; rep from * around; join in 3rd ch of beg ch-3. *(44 dc)*

Rnd 5: Ch 3, dc in next 2 dc, 2 dc in next dc; *dc in next 3 dc, 2 dc in next dc; rep from * around; join in 3rd ch of beg ch-3. *(55 dc)*

Rnd 6: Ch 3, dc in next 3 dc, 2 dc in next dc; *dc in next 4 dc, 2 dc in next dc; rep from * around; join in 3rd ch of beg ch-3. *(66 dc)*

Rnd 7: Ch 3, dc in next 4 dc, 2 dc in next dc; *dc in next 5 dc, 2 dc in next dc; rep from * around; join in 3rd ch of beg ch-3. *(77 dc)*

Rnd 8: Ch 3, dc in next 5 dc, 2 dc in next dc; *dc in next 6 dc, 2 dc in next dc; rep from * around; join in 3rd ch of beg ch-3. *(88 dc)*

Rnd 9: Ch 3, dc in next 6 dc, 2 dc in next dc; *dc in next 7 dc, 2 dc in next dc; rep from * around; join in 3rd ch of beg ch-3. *(99 dc)*

Rnd 10: Ch 3, dc in next 7 dc, 2 dc in next dc; *dc in next 8 dc, 2 dc in next dc; rep from * around; join in 3rd ch of beg ch-3. *(110 dc)*

Rnd 11: Ch 3, dc in next 8 dc, 2 dc in next dc; *dc in next 9 dc, 2 dc in next dc; rep from * around; join in 3rd ch of beg ch-3. *(121 dc)*

Rnd 12: Ch 3, dc in next 9 dc, 2 dc in next dc; *dc in next 10 dc, 2 dc in next dc; rep from * around; join in 3rd ch of beg ch-3. *(132 dc)*

Rnd 13: Ch 3, dc in next 10 dc, 2 dc in next dc; *dc in next 11 dc, 2 dc in next dc; rep from * around; join in 3rd ch of beg ch-3. *(143 dc)*

Rnd 14: Ch 3, dc in next 11 dc, 2 dc in next dc; *dc in next 12 dc, 2 dc in next dc; rep from * around; join in 3rd ch of beg ch-3. *(154 dc)*

Rnd 15: Ch 3, dc in next 12 dc, 2 dc in next dc; *dc in next 13 dc, 2 dc in next dc; rep from * around; join in 3rd ch of beg ch-3. *(165 dc)*

Rnd 16: Ch 3, dc in next 13 dc, 2 dc in next dc; *dc in next 14 dc, 2 dc in next dc; rep from * around; join in 3rd ch of beg ch-3. *(176 dc)*

Rnd 17: Ch 3, dc in next 14 dc, 2 dc in next dc; *dc in next 15 dc, 2 dc in next dc; rep from * around; join in 3rd ch of beg ch-3. *(187 dc)*

Rnd 18: Ch 3, dc in next 15 dc, 2 dc in next dc; *dc in next 16 dc, 2 dc in next dc; rep from * around; join in 3rd ch of beg ch-3. *(198 dc)*

Rnd 19: Ch 3, dc in next 16 dc, 2 dc in next dc; *dc in next 17 dc, 2 dc in next dc; rep from * around; join in 3rd ch of beg ch-3. *(209 dc)*

Rnd 20: Ch 3, dc in next 17 dc, 2 dc in next dc; *dc in next 18 dc, 2 dc in next dc; rep from * around; join in 3rd ch of beg ch-3. *(220 dc)*

Rnd 21: Ch 3, dc in next 18 dc, 2 dc in next dc; *dc in next 19 dc, 2 dc in next dc; rep from * around; join in 3rd ch of beg ch-3. *(231 dc)*

Rnd 22: Ch 3, dc in next 19 dc, 2 dc in next dc; *dc in next 20 dc, 2 dc in next dc; rep from * around; join in 3rd ch of beg ch-3. *(242 dc)*

Fasten off B only and join C.

Rnd 23: Ch 3, dc in next 20 dc, 2 dc in next dc; *dc in next 21 dc, 2 dc in next dc; rep from * around; join in 3rd ch of beg ch-3. *(253 dc)*

Rnd 24: Ch 3, dc in next 21 dc, 2 dc in next dc; *dc in next 22 dc, 2 dc in next dc; rep from * around; join in 3rd ch of beg ch-3. *(264 dc)*

Rnd 25: Ch 3, dc in next 22 dc, 2 dc in next dc; *dc in next 23 dc, 2 dc in next dc; rep from * around; join in 3rd ch of beg ch-3. *(275 dc)*

Fasten off C only and join D.

Rnd 26: Ch 3, dc in next 23 dc, 2 dc in next dc; *dc in next 24 dc, 2 dc in next dc; rep from * around; join in 3rd ch of beg ch-3. *(286 dc)*

Rnd 27: Ch 3, dc in next 24 dc, 2 dc in next dc; *dc in next 25 dc, 2 dc in next dc; rep from * around; join in 3rd ch of beg ch-3. *(297 dc)*

Rnd 28: Ch 3, dc in next 25 dc, 2 dc in next dc; *dc in next 26 dc, 2 dc in next dc; rep from * around; join in 3rd ch of beg ch-3. *(308 dc)*

Fasten off and weave in all ends.

Felting

Note: *Refer to How to Felt on page 1 for additional information.*

Wash by machine on a hot wash/cold rinse cycle with detergent and several pieces of clothing to agitate. To felt additionally, dry by machine on a regular setting until almost dry. Remove from dryer and pull into shape.

EASY

Finished Size

Approximately 14 x 14 inches after felting; size will vary depending on amount of felting

Materials

- Lion Brand Fishermen's Wool medium (worsted) weight yarn (8 oz/465 yds/117 g) per skein:
  2 skeins #098 natural *(A)*
- Lion Brand Fun Fur bulky (chunky) weight yarn (1¾ oz/60yds/50g) per ball:
  6 balls #133 tangerine or #211 Hawaii *(B)*
- Size N/13/9mm crochet hook or size needed to obtain gauge
- Tapestry needle
- 14 x 14 inch pillow form

4 MEDIUM

5 BULKY

Gauge

With 1 strand of A and B held tog: 8 dc = 4 inches

Instructions

Front/Back

Make 2.

Rnd 1 (RS): With 1 strand each of A and B held tog, ch 4; join to form a ring; ch 5 *(counts as a dc and ch-2-sp on this and following rnds)*, [2 dc in ring, ch 2] 3 times; dc in ring; join in 3rd ch of beg ch-5. *(8 dc)*

Rnd 2: Sl st in next ch-2 sp, ch 5, 2 dc in same sp—*beg corner made;* *dc in next 2 dc; in next ch-2 sp work (2 dc, ch 2, 2 dc)—corner made;* rep from * twice; dc in next dc, in joining sl st of previous rnd and in same ch-2 sp as beg ch-5 made; join in 3rd ch of beg ch-5.

Rnd 2: Sl st in next ch-2 sp, beg corner in same sp; *dc in each dc to next corner ch-2 sp; corner in corner ch-2 sp; rep from * twice more; dc in each rem dc, in joining sl st of previous rnd and in same ch-2 sp as beg ch-5 made; join in 3rd ch of beg ch-5.

Rnds 3–12: Rep rnd 2.

Fasten off and weave in all ends.

Assembly

Hold pieces with RS tog; working through both pieces at same time and with 1 strand of A and B held tog, make slip knot on hook and join with sc in any corner ch-2 sp; ch 1, 3 sc in same sp; sc evenly spaced around pieces, working 3 sc in each rem corner ch-2 sp, until 3 sides are joined. Fasten off and weave in ends. Turn RS out.

Felting

Note: *Refer to How to Felt on page 1 for additional information.*

Wash by machine on a hot wash/cold rinse cycle with detergent and several pieces of clothing to agitate. To felt additionally, dry by machine on a regular setting until almost dry. Remove from dryer and pull into shape.

Finishing

Insert pillow form and sew remaining side closed.

Furry Hat

EASY

Finished Sizes

Instructions given fit adult size 20-inch head circumference *(small)*; changes for adult size 22-inch head circumference *(medium)* are in [ ].

Finished Garment Measurements

Circumference after felting: approximately 22 inches *(small)* [23½ inches *(medium)*]; size will vary depending on amount of felting

Materials

• Lion Brand Lion Wool medium (worsted) weight yarn (3 oz/158 yds/85g per ball): 1 ball #153 ebony *(A)*
• Lion Brand Fun Fur bulky (chunky) weight yarn (1¾ oz/60 yds/50g) per ball: 2 balls #126 chocolate *(B)*
• Sizes N/13/9mm crochet hook or size needed to obtain gauge
• Tapestry needle

Gauge

9½ sc = 4 inches before felting

Instructions

Rnd 1: With 1 strand of A and B held tog, ch 3; join to form a ring; ch 1, 8 sc in ring; join in first sc.

Rnd 2: Ch 1, 2 sc in same sc and in each rem sc; join in first sc. *(16 sc)*

Rnd 3: Ch 1, sc in same sc, 2 sc in next sc; *sc in next sc, 2 sc in next sc; rep from * around; join with in first sc. *(24 sc)*

Rnd 4: Ch 1, sc in same sc and in next sc, 2 sc in next sc; *sc in next 2 sc, 2 sc in next sc; rep from * around; join in first sc. *(32 sc)*

Rnd 5: Ch 1, sc in same sc and in next 2 sc, 2 sc in next sc; *sc in next 3 sc, 2 sc in next sc; rep from * around; join in first sc. *(40 sc)*

Rnd 6: Ch 1, sc in same sc and in next 3 sc, 2 sc in next sc; *sc in next 4 sc, 2 sc in next sc; rep from * around; join in first sc. *(48 sc)*

Rnd 7: Ch 1, sc in same sc and in next 4 sc, 2 sc in next sc; *sc in next 5 sc, 2 sc in next sc; rep from * around; join in first sc. *(56 sc)*

Rnd 8: Ch 1, sc in same sc and in next 12 [5] sc, 2 sc in next sc; *sc in next 13 [6] sc, 2 sc in next sc; rep from * around; join in first sc. *(60 [64] sc)*

Rnd 9: Ch 1, sc in same sc and in each rem sc; join in first sc, turn.

Rnd 10 (WS): Ch 1, sc in same sc and in each rem sc; join in first sc; turn.

Rnds 11–20 (11–22): [Work rows 9 and 10] 5 [6] times.

Rnds 21 (23): Rep rnd 9.

Fasten off and weave in all ends.

Felting

***Note:** Refer to How to Felt on page 1 for additional information.*

Turn RS out. Wash by machine on a hot wash/cold rinse cycle with detergent and several pieces of clothing to agitate. To felt additionally, dry by machine on a regular setting until almost dry. Remove from dryer and pull into shape.

Child's Cap

EASY

Finished Sizes

Instructions are given for child's size 4; changes for sizes 6 and 8 are in [ ].

Finished Garment Measurements

Circumference: approximately 18½ [19½, 20½] inches after felting; size will vary depending on amount of felting

Materials

Version A:
• Lion Brand Lion Wool medium (worsted) weight yarn (3 oz/158 yds/85g per ball): 1 ball each #123 sage *(A)* and #204 majestic mountain *(B)*
• Size I/9/5.5mm crochet hook or size needed to obtain gauge
•Tapestry needle

Version B:
• Lion Brand Lion Wool medium (worsted) weight yarn (3 oz/158 yds/85g per ball): 1 ball each #140 rose *(A)* and #202 flower garden *(B)*
• Size I/9/5.5mm crochet hook or size needed to obtain gauge
•Tapestry needle

Gauge

12 sc = 4 inches before felting

Instructions

Cap

Rnd 1: With A, ch 3; join to form a ring; ch 1, 8 sc in ring; join in first sc.

Rnd 2: Ch 1, 2 sc in each sc; join in first sc. *(16 sc)*

Rnd 3: Ch 1, sc in same sc; 2 sc in next sc; *sc in next sc, 2 sc in next sc; rep from * around; join in first sc. *(24 sc)*

Rnd 4: Ch 1, sc in same sc and in next sc; 2 sc in next sc; *sc in next 2 sc, 2 sc in next sc; rep from * around; join in first sc. *(32 sc)*

Rnd 5: Ch 1, sc in same sc and in next 2 sc; 2 sc in next sc; *sc in next 3 sc, 2 sc in next sc; rep from * around; join in first sc. *(40 sc)*

Rnd 6: Ch 1, sc in same sc and in next 3 sc, 2 sc in next sc; *sc in next 4 sc, 2 sc in next sc; rep from * around; join in first sc. *(48 sc)*

Rnd 7: Ch 1, sc in same sc and in next 4 sc; *sc in next 5 sc, 2 sc in next sc; rep from * around; join in first sc. *(56 sc)*

Rnd 8: Ch 1, sc in same sc and in next 12 [5, 5] sc, 2 sc in next sc; *sc in next 13 [6, 6] sc, 2 sc in next sc; rep from * around; join in first sc. *(60 [64, 64] sc)*

For Sizes 4 & 6 Only

Continue with Edging.

For Size 8 Only

Rnd 9: Ch 1, sc in same sc and in next 14 sc, 2 sc in next sc; *sc in next 15 sc, 2 sc in next sc; rep from * around; join in first sc. *(68 sc)*

Continue with Edging.

Edging

Row 1 (RS): Ch 1, sc in same sc and in each rem sc; join in first sc, turn. *(60 [64, 68] sc)*

Row 2: Ch 1, sc in same sc and in each rem sc; join in first sc, turn.

For Size 4 Only

Rows 3–5: Rep row 2. At end of row 5, change to B by drawing lp through; cut A.

Rows 6–10: Rep row 2.

At end of row 10, change to A; cut B.

Rows 11-15: Rep row 2.

Fasten off and weave in all ends.

For Size 6 Only

Rows 3–6: Rep row 2. At end of row 6, change to B by drawing lp through; cut A.

Rows 7–12: Rep row 2.

At end of row 12, change to A; cut B.

Rows 13-18: Rep row 2.

Fasten off and weave in all ends.

For Size 8 Only

Rows 3–7: Rep row 2. At end of row 7, change to B by drawing lp through; cut A.

Rows 8–14: Rep row 2.

At end of row 14, change to A; cut B.

Rows 15-21: Rep row 2.

Fasten off and weave in all ends.

Felting

Note: *Refer to How to Felt on page 1 for additional information.*

Turn Cap RS out. Wash by machine on a hot wash/cold rinse cycle with detergent and several pieces of clothing to agitate. To felt additionally, dry by machine on a regular setting until almost dry. Remove from dryer and pull into shape.

Clever Containers

EASY

Finished Sizes

Container A: approximately 7½ x 7½ x 7½ inches after felting

Container B: approximately 7 x 7 x 8½ inches after felting

Container C: approximately 7½ x 2½ x 4 inches after felting

Sizes will vary depending on amount of felting.

Materials

- Lion Brand Lion Wool medium (worsted) weight yarn (3 oz/158 yds/85g per ball):
  5 balls #099 winter white *(A)*
  4 balls #123 sage *(B)*
  3 balls #133 pumpkin *(C)*
- Size J/10/6mm crochet hook or size needed to obtain gauge
- Tapestry needle

Gauge

15 sc = 4 inches before felting

Instructions

Container A

Bottom

Row 1 (RS): With B, ch 45; sc in 2nd ch from hook and in each rem ch, turn.

Row 2: Ch 1, sc in each sc, turn.

Rows 3–49: Rep row 2.

Container A

Row 50: Ch 1, sc in each sc.

Fasten off and weave in ends.

Side

Make 4.

Row 1 (RS): With B, ch 45; sc in 2nd ch from hook and in each rem ch, turn.

Row 2: Ch 1, sc in each sc, turn.

Rows 3–24: Rep row 2. At end of row 24, change to C by drawing lp through; cut B.

Rows 25–36: Rep row 2. At end of row 36, change to A; cut C.

Rows 37–48: Rep row 2. At end of row 48, change to B; cut C.

Row 49: Ch 1, sc in each sc.

Fasten off and weave in all ends.

Container B

Bottom

Row 1 (RS): With A, ch 35; sc in 2nd ch from hook and in each rem ch, turn. *(34 sc)*

Row 2: Ch 1, sc in each sc, turn.

Rows 3–40: Rep row 2.

Fasten off and weave in ends.

Side

Make 4.

Row 1 (RS): With A, ch 35; sc in 2nd ch from hook and in each rem ch, turn. *(34 sc)*

Row 2: Ch 1, sc in each sc, turn.

Container B

Container C

Rows 3–40: Rep row 2. At end of row 40, change to C by drawing lp through; cut A.

Rows 41–48: Rep row 2. At end of row 48, change to B by drawing lp through; cut C.

Rows 49–56: Rep row 2. At end of row 56, change to A by drawing lp through; cut B.

Row 57: Ch 1, sc in each sc.

Fasten off and weave in all ends.

Container C
Bottom

Row 1 (RS): With C, ch 45; sc in 2nd ch from hook and in each rem ch, turn. *(44 sc)*

Row 2: Ch 1, sc in each sc, turn.

Rows 3–12: Rep row 2.

Fasten off and weave in ends.

Long Side
Make 2.

Row 1 (RS): With C, ch 45; sc in 2nd ch from hook and in each rem ch, turn. *(44 sc)*

Row 2: Ch 1, sc in each sc, turn.

Rows 3–18: Rep row 2. At end of row 18, change to A by drawing lp through; cut C.

Rows 19–22: Rep row 2. At end of row 22, change to B by drawing lp through; cut A.

Rows 23–26: Rep row 2. At end of row 26, change to C by drawing lp through; cut B.

Row 27: Ch 1, sc in each sc.

Fasten off and weave in all ends.

Short Side
Make 2.

Row 1 (RS): With C, ch 11; sc in 2nd ch from hook and in each rem ch, turn. *(10 sc)*

Row 2: Ch 1, sc in each sc, turn.

Rows 3–18: Rep row 2. At end of row 18, change to A by drawing lp through; cut C.

Rows 19–22: Rep row 2. At end of row 22, change to B by drawing lp through; cut A.

Rows 23–26: Rep row 2. At end of row 26, change to C by drawing lp through; cut B.

Row 27: Ch 1, sc in each sc.

Fasten off and weave in all ends.

Assembly
With WS facing you, matching stripes, and with matching color, join sides tog with sc to form box. Join bottom to sides with sc. Turn RS out.

Felting
***Note:** Refer to How to Felt on page 1 for additional information.*

Wash by machine on a hot wash/cold rinse cycle with detergent and several pieces of clothing to agitate. To felt additionally, dry by machine on a regular setting until almost dry. Remove from dryer and pull into shape.

EASY

Finished Sizes

Instructions given fit size small; changes for medium and large are in [ ].

Finished Garment Measurements

Circumference: approximately 20 [22, 24] inches after felting; size will vary depending on amount of felting

Materials

- Lion Brand Bolero super bulky (super chunky) weight yarn (3½ oz/55 yds/100g per skein):
  3 (3, 4) skeins #203 hazelnut
- Size Q/15mm crochet hook or size needed to obtain gauge
- Tapestry needle

SUPER BULKY

Gauge

10 sc = 6 inches

Instructions

Rnd 1: Loosely ch 42 [46, 50]; join to form a ring, being careful not to twist chs; ch 1, sc in same ch as joining and in each rem ch; join in first sc. *(42 [46, 50] sc)*

Rep rnd 1 until piece measures 8 inches from beg.

Crown Shaping

For Size Small Only

*Note: For **sc dec**, draw up lp in each of 2 sts indicated, yo and draw through all 3 lps on hook.*

Rnd 1: Ch 1, sc in same sc and in next 3 sc; ***sc dec** (see Note)* in next 2 sts; sc in next 4 sc; rep from * to last 2 sc; sc dec in last 2 sc; join in first sc. *(35 sc)*

Rnd 2: Ch 1, sc in same sc and in each rem sc; join in first sc.

Rnd 3: Ch 1, sc in same sc and in next 2 sc; *sc dec; sc in next 3 sc; rep from * to last 2 sc; sc dec; join in first sc. *(28 sc)*

Rnd 4: Rep rnd 2.

Rnd 5: Ch 1, sc in same sc and in next sc; *sc dec; sc in next 2 sc; rep from * to last 2 sc; sc dec; join in first sc. *(21 sc)*

Rnd 6: Ch 1, sc in same sc; *sc dec; sc in next sc; rep from * to last 2 sc; sc dec; join in first sc. *(14 sc)*

Rnd 7: Ch 1, [sc dec] 7 times; join in first sc. *(7 sc)*

Fasten off, leaving 8-inch end for sewing.

With tapestry needle and long end, sew center hole closed. Weave in ends.

For Size Medium Only

*Note: For **sc dec**, draw up lp in each of 2 sts indicated, yo and draw through all 3 lps on hook.*

Rnd 1: Ch 1, sc in same sc and in next 3 sc; ***sc dec** (see Note)* in next 2 sts; sc in next 3 sc; rep from * to last 2 sc; sc dec in last 2 sc; join in first sc. *(37 sc)*

Rnd 2: Ch 1, sc in each sc; join in first sc.

Rnd 3: Ch 1, sc in same sc and in next 7 sc; *sc dec; sc in next 7 sc; rep from * to last 2 sc; sc dec; join in first sc. *(33 sc)*

Rnd 4: Rep rnd 2.

Rnd 5: Ch 1, sc in same sc and in next 2 sc; *sc dec; sc in next 2 sc; rep from * to last 2 sc; sc dec; join in first sc. *(25 sc)*

Rnd 6: Ch 1, sc in same sc and in next sc; *sc dec; sc in next sc; rep from * to last 2 sc; sc dec; join in first sc. *(17 sc)*

Rnd 7: Ch 1, sc in same sc; [sc dec] 8 times; join in first sc. *(9 sc)*

Fasten off, leaving 8-inch end for sewing.

With tapestry needle and long end, sew center hole closed. Weave in ends.

For Size Large Only

*Note: For **sc dec**, draw up lp in each of 2 sts indicated, yo and draw through all 3 lps on hook.*

Rnd 1: Ch 1, sc in same sc; *sc in next 5 sc, **sc dec** (see Note) in next 2 sc; rep from * around; join in first sc. *(43 sc)*

Rnd 2: Ch 1, sc in each sc; join in first sc.

Rnd 3: Ch 1, sc in same sc and in next 4 sc; *sc dec; sc in next 4 sc; rep from * to last 2 sc; sc dec; join in first sc. *(36 sc)*

Rnd 4: Ch 1, sc in each sc; join in first sc.

Rnd 5: Ch 1, sc in same sc and in next 3 sc; *sc dec; sc in next 3 sc; rep from * to last 2 sc; sc dec; join in first sc. *(29 sc)*

Rnd 6: Rep rnd 4.

Rnd 7: Ch 1, sc in same sc and in next 2 sc; *sc dec; sc in next 2 sc; rep from * to last 2 sc; sc dec; join in first sc. *(22 sc)*

Rnd 8: Ch 1, sc in same sc and in next sc; *sc dec; sc in next sc; rep from * to last 2 sc; sc dec; join in first sc. *(15 sc)*

Rnd 9: Ch 1, sc in same sc; [sc dec] 7 times; join in first sc. *(8 sc)*

Fasten off, leaving 8-inch end for sewing.

With tapestry needle and long end, sew center hole closed. Weave in ends.

Flower

Ch 3; join to form a ring; *ch 4, sc in 2nd ch from hook, hdc in next 2 chs, sl st in ring; rep from * 4 times more. Fasten off.

Felting

Note: *Refer to How to Felt on page 1 for additional information.*

Turn RS out. Place pieces in washing machine. Wash on a hot wash/cold rinse cycle with detergent and several pieces of clothing to agitate. Pull hat into shape, turn up brim, and let air dry.

Finishing

With tapestry needle, sew Flower to Cloche.

Standard Yarn Weight System

Categories of yarn, gauge ranges, and recommended needle and hook sizes

Yarn Weight Symbol & Category Names	1 SUPER FINE	2 FINE	3 LIGHT	4 MEDIUM	5 BULKY	6 SUPER BULKY
Type of Yarns in Category	Sock, Fingering, Baby	Sport, Baby	DK, Light Worsted	Worsted, Afghan, Aran	Chunky, Craft, Rug	Bulky, Roving
Crochet Gauge* Ranges in Single Crochet to 4 inch	21–32 sts	16–20 sts	12–17 sts	11–14 sts	8–11 sts	5–9 sts
Recommended Hook in Metric Size Range	2.25–3.5 mm	3.5–4.5 mm	4.5–5.5 mm	5.5–6.5 mm	6.5–9 mm	9 mm and larger
Recommended Hook U.S. Size Range	B1–E4	E4–7	7–I-9	I-9–K-10½	K-10½–M-13	M-13 and larger

* GUIDELINES ONLY: The above reflect the most commonly used gauges and hook sizes for specific yarn categories.

Abbreviations & Symbols

beg .... begin/beginning
bpdc .... back post double crochet
bpsc .... back post single crochet
bptr ....back post treble crochet
CC .... contrasting color
ch.. chain stitch
ch- ....refers to chain or space previously made (i.e. ch-1 space)
ch sp .... chain space
cl.. cluster
cm ....centimeter(s)
dc ....double crochet
dc dec ....double crochet 2 or more stitches together, as indicated
dec .... decrease/decreases/decreasing
dtr..double treble crochet
fpdc...front post double crochet
fpsc ....front post single crochet
fptr ....front post treble crochet
g ....grams
hdc .... half double crochet
hdc dec... half double crochet 2 or more stitches together, as indicated
lp(s) ....loops(s)
MC .... main color
mm ....millimeter(s)
oz..ounce(s)
pc .... popcorn
rem .... remain/remaining
rep...repeat(s)
rnd(s) .... round(s)
RS ....right side
sc..single crochet
sc dec............single crochet 2 or more stitches together, as indicated
sk.. skip
sl st...slip stitch
sp(s) ....space(s)
st(s) .... stitch(es)

tog.. together
tr... treble crochet
trtr ....triple treble
WS .... wrong side
yd(s)..yard(s)
yo .... yarn over

* An asterisk (or double asterisk **) is used to mark the beginning of a portion of instructions to be worked more than once; thus, "rep from * twice more" means after working the instructions once, repeat the instructions following the asterisk twice more (3 times in all).

[] Brackets are used to enclose instructions that should be worked the exact number of times specified immediately following the brackets, such as "[2 sc in next dc, sc in next dc] twice." They are also used to set off and clarify a group of stitches that are to be worked all into the same space or stitch, such as "in next corner sp work [2 dc, ch 1, 2 dc]."

[] Brackets and () parentheses are used to provide additional information to clarify instructions.

Join—join with a sl st unless otherwise specified.

The patterns in this book are written using United States terminology. Terms that have different British equivalents are noted below.

U.S. Terms	U.K. Terms
single crochet (sc)	double crochet (dc)
double crochet (dc)	treble (tr)
treble crochet (tr)	double treble (dtr)
skip (sk)	miss
slip stitch (sl st)	slip stitch (ss) or single crochet
gauge	tension
yarn over (yo)	yarn over hook (YOH)

How to Check Gauge

A correct stitch gauge is very important. Please take the time to work a stitch gauge swatch about 4 x 4 inches. Measure the swatch. If the number of stitches and rows are fewer than indicated under "Gauge" in the pattern, your hook is too large. Try another swatch with a smaller size hook. If the number of stitches and rows are more than indicated under "Gauge" in the pattern, your hook is too small. Try another swatch with a larger size hook.

Stitch Guide

Chain—ch:
YO, draw through lp on hook.

Single Crochet—sc:
Insert hook in st, yo and draw through, yo and draw through both lps on hook.

Reverse Single Crochet—Reverse sc:
Work from left to right, insert hook in sp or st indicated (**a**), draw lp through sp or st - 2 lps on hook (**b**); yo and draw through lps on hook.

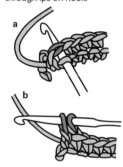

Half Double Crochet—hdc:
yo, insert hook in st, yo, draw through, yo and draw through all 3 lps on hook.

Double Crochet—dc:
yo, insert hook in st, yo, draw through, (yo and draw through 2 lps on hook) twice.

Triple Crochet—trc:
yo twice, insert hook in st, yo, draw through, (yo and draw through 2 lps on hook) 3 times.

Slip Stitch—sl st:
(a) Used for Joinings
Insert hook in indicated st, yo and draw through st and lp on hook.

(b) Used for Moving Yarn Over
Insert hook in st, yo draw through st and lp on hook.

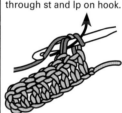

Front Loop—FL:
The front loop is the loop toward you at the top of the stitch.

Back Loop—BL:
The back loop is the loop away from you at the top of the stitch.

Post:
The post is the vertical part of the stitch.

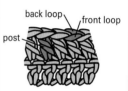

Overcast Stitch is worked loosely to join crochet pieces.

Skill Levels

BEGINNER
Beginner projects for first-time crocheters using basic stitches. Minimal shaping.

EASY
Easy projects using basic stitches, repetitive stitch patterns, simple color changes and simple shaping and finishing.

INTERMEDIATE
Intermediate projects with a variety of stitches, mid-level shaping and finishing.

EXPERIENCED
Experienced projects using advanced techniques and stitches, detailed shaping and refined finishing.

INCHES INTO MILLIMETERS & CENTIMETERS (Rounded off slightly)

inches	mm	cm	inches	cm	inches	cm	inches	cm
1/8	3	0.3	5	12.5	21	53.5	38	96.5
1/4	6	0.6	5 1/2	14	22	56	39	99
3/8	10	1	6	15	23	58.5	40	101.5
1/2	13	1.3	7	18	24	61	41	104
5/8	15	1.5	8	20.5	25	63.5	42	106.5
3/4	20	2	9	23	26	66	43	109
7/8	22	2.2	10	25.5	27	68.5	44	112
1	25	2.5	11	28	28	71	45	114.5
1 1/4	32	3.2	12	30.5	29	73.5	46	117
1 1/2	38	3.8	13	33	30	76	47	119.5
1 3/4	45	4.5	14	35.5	31	79	48	122
2	50	5	15	38	32	81.5	49	124.5
2 1/2	65	6.5	16	40.5	33	84	50	127
3	75	7.5	17	43	34	86.5		
3 1/2	90	9	18	46	35	89		
4	100	10	19	48.5	36	91.5		
4 1/2	115	11.5	20	51	37	94		

CROCHET HOOKS CONVERSION CHART

U.S.	1/B	2/C	3/D	4/E	5/F	6/G	8/H	9/I	10/J	10½/K	N
Continental-mm	2.25	2.75	3.25	3.5	3.75	4.25	5	5.5	6	6.5	9.0

American School of Needlework®
excellence in instruction

DRG Publishing
306 East Parr Road
Berne, IN 46711
©2006 American School of Needlework

TOLL-FREE ORDER LINE or to request a free catalog (800) 582-6643
Customer Service (800) 282-6643, **Fax** (800) 882-6643

Visit AnniesAttic.com.

We have made every effort to ensure the accuracy and completeness of these instructions.
We cannot, however, be responsible for human error, typographical mistakes or variations in individual work.

ISBN-10: 1-59012-168-6   All rights reserved.   Printed in USA   1 2 3 4 5 6 7 8 9
ISBN-13: 978-1-59012-168-9